COMMA

COMMA · Jennifer Still

FIRST EDITION

Copyright ©2017 Jennifer Still

All rights reserved.
No part of this publication may be reproduced or transmitted in any form or by any means, electronic or mechanical, including photocopying, recording, or any information storage or retrieval system, without permission in writing from the publishers.

Cover and interior by Beautiful Outlaw

WWW.BOOKTHUG.CA

The production of this book was made possible through the generous assistance of the Canada Council for the Arts and the Ontario Arts Council. BookThug also acknowledges the support of the Government of Canada through the Canada Book Fund and the Government of Ontario through the Ontario Book Publishing Tax Credit and the Ontario Book Fund.

LIBRARY AND ARCHIVES CANADA CATALOGUING IN PUBLICATION

Still, Jennifer, 1973– , author
    Comma/ Jennifer Still. – First Edition
Poems.

Issued in print and electronic formats.
SOFTCOVER: ISBN 978-1-77166-310-6
HTML: ISBN 978-1-77166-311-3
PDF: ISBN 978-1-77166-312-0
KINDLE: ISBN 978-1-77166-313-7

    I. Title.

PS8637.T54C66 2017   C811'.6   C2017-900350-X | C2017-900351-8

PRINTED IN CANADA

Contents

CHRYSALIS

SECTION I · COMMON BLUE

SECTION II · SCROLL

SECTION III · SWARM

SECTION IV · PAPERY ACTS

SECTION V · THORN

SECTION VI · GRIEF SILHOUETTES

SECTION VII · COMMA

Fragments are the husk of a secret.
Mary Ruefle

CHRYSALIS

Back and back we leaned
on what we thought we were. The light
went and childhood came off. The hook
between *chance* and *change* left a worm
threaded to the glass. Silence. You are
the specimen. Was it glue peeled
from our fingertips or maybe sadness
hadn't finished itself? Somewhere
just below the breath, silence
reorders: listen to the ink flap
lappet lappet, the rip inside water
when my fingernail strikes the tank.
You said it was like thunder, my light
tap on the glass, and I believe in every touch
I can't yet hear. *I sit quietly at my desk. Scraps
of sounds work into something*: tetra scatter
at the window, stars parting, the open
shred. You are turning back
into yourself. A paper curled around
the finger, still shaped to the body,
the body, a fragment impossibly small
for the span. You will become
a line, bent, on your own tiny
sun. An antennae fastened
to the rustle in the air. Take this breath.
Do you hear it? Wriggling right out
of its ending: There is *praise* in *respiration*.
There is *repair*.

SECTION I · COMMON BLUE

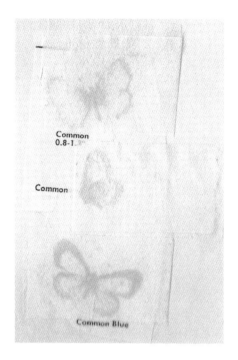

.

time fused   the underside
pale

              honeydew

.

of   viscous
              quality

your
glueface

TONGUE in a blue gown

asks
for a COKE

The poem is self-adhesive

hinge]   The hook on which a door
                              turns
                       fig.
                 depends

Its main use :
hinging light

.

BLUE-DEVILS   n.
pl.   A colloquial phrase for dejection   hypo-
         lowness of spirits   also for *de-
lirium tremens*

                                       The name of

.

the last hue to print
when the toner runs dry

the dawn we all bleed to

BLUES are small and usually
          secret

.

TAILED BLUE
                              its range
      to fall
several generations   early

.

WAR BLUE is similar but lacks
our faces at the end of

your trigger

.

MY BLUE
the smallest of all
                its
well-
      camouflaged
tongue

OTHER FAMILIES
OTHER   LIES

(you were

often absent.
p ISS

                    p.155
              looks like *PISS*)

OTHER
      LIES

    turn dark

turn

.

     -self

They need
shade and reason

.

      let) let
 lilac
          (where you crouch inside

   this

   tiny WILD

THE SECRET comes out
of its long

shade

.

<pre>
GRASS   star

low center   borne atop
                        The narrow
lying
             Blue-eye   thrives in
         moist meadow and open

                            Family
</pre>

DAYS
PASSED

        (on the ground

the pupa resembled

.

a face   :

TO GROW

        to grow

        in many forms

.

simple   blue

        downwards

    -tinged

.

ANTENNARIA NEGLECTA

                white wool

                      disc

              heart
                        halfway to

                pearly everlasting

.

          what to do with the
old skins these

       grayish

        papery
                    acts

BLOOD   The

     long

         lower
    milk

         a first
               flower

shaded

             tended by
the ~~upperside~~
   underside

      several generations

.

~~Blue~~
Blur

               to
               dim
               dim

~~ononaria, or lowness of spirits; also~~ de-lirium ~~tremens. Often called simply~~ *the*

STRONGER POINTS   Developed

by   ear
)   Art   To participate in creating

       meaning

Prove every Turquoise
lead will make a distinct black line
well over 35 miles long

.

(There are 50,000–100,000
venous miles in the human body

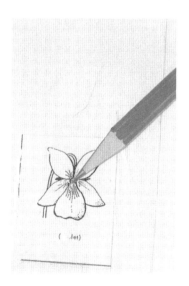

SANGUINARIA

 eyerings   whiteflower   anaemic
(everings)

iceplant   ghostflower   Indian Pipe

.

-let
           ink
pose

sanginarius means bleeding

.

the fleshy
           lack

structural color can be

The combination of

eyes

blue eyes,   blue
Blue   eyes

blue   a physical color.

SPLENDOR OF IRIS

The choice of
happy   was probably

                    chemical
caused by

.

                    those whose

glass
        contained

the   ability to reflect

.

On clear days
    water droplets

spheric layers   part
particle
        (Anything

    scattering varies

    a standard
    light ray

.

The smaller
    complex
good

CHANGE IS ONLY NATURAL

  How does the feather produce blue? To understand understand

           why the sky

the principle first outlined
      does not fade

under the 500 mile-long strokes
        of a hummingbird's

    pencil eraser heart

EVERY PARTICLE

of graphite glides

(It would take 70,000 chemi-sealed Turquoise
 pencils

to draw you

into a solid unit
at a rare axis

.

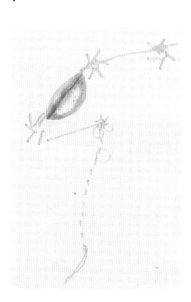

TO RESIST POINT

breakage

follow the blank

                        in the sky

HEAVENLY BLUE

                of the newly developed
(eye   or worm-
                              glisten
     or bright
united
    us   rolling
             (Wild   or Glory   twining
                             persistent
                                                  as far
                  as   summer
                                  or
                  purple throat

                  heart-*sh*   If you want to
on this page   you can let your
                        rose
              along
       rows

                       arrow-*sh*
                       and bell-*sh*

         over   the   over
                       Glory   root
        The funnel
    long   or pink or pale

GENTIANS

to close this
                              blár
connect   with *blow*   a blow
kin
                    to what is blue
                    to dye of a blue

.

era   ear   Gentiana   generation
                  acaulis
                  a call is

.

~~tian)~~   1 to 2 ft.
scarcely opening

solitary

(so lit

TO END ON

trumpets
blue   closed bell-

            trumpets

                    with ink   and
                common   call

your house and garden   cell
the continuous

WAR

comes out
of its long

habit

cocks a
finger

funnels to
⠀⠀⠀⠀blue

.

let blue

⠀lower⠀⠀its second

ear
(The bottle
⠀⠀⠀⠀⠀⠀⠀⠀⠀⠀⠀⠀⠀⠀⠀resembles
⠀⠀⠀⠀⠀a root
⠀⠀⠀⠀⠀⠀⠀⠀⠀⠀⠀within

and should be picked
with

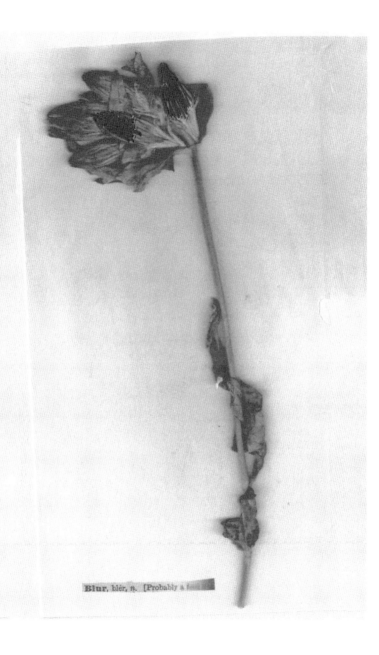

.

the ends of   a
            split

.

pen

GROW

    flower

                allow
               habit
      its site on the stem

lusters   divide   wet meadows

The tiny seeds   cap

.

for an
easy end   All we want
    tied
         to a long

blue salve
       meter   The veined
                          Flow-

SECTION II · SCROLL

DERMA, DREAM

I ate everything but the skin. Which was tough, mom's
licorice. The snake slipped out of its hole, a childhood
choke. Under the private weight of sleep, the canvas walls
flapped. *Were you scared when you first saw it?* Mostly
we were at home, behind a curtain, at the hem of stars.
There was a worm caught up in my gums, an amoebic
mouth. I held your pillow to my face and
a scent. *What is brave?* The wrinkle peeling off
the undersheet. The page taking forty years
to blush, to publish
light. *Is there a blind feeling when it comes?*
A collapse of warm air. Like a trouser sock, or a hose.
There was a shimmer in the hay. A crease in the allotted
breath. We tilted the blinds. The stars folded in.
And I remembered in amazement that I could swallow, and I did.

GOBSTOPPER

In the small mirror where my red face floats.
I can still see it, the egg on the sidewalk that makes me
look up to the hole in the throat. Behind every word
there's a socket in the night where our dove flew out.
What is private? In the rearview where all our red faces
float. Here, between colours, we have been stopped
for such a long time. All the engines are cooing
while she is being hit from the inside. Her pale arms
chop. I can see right through to the tiny *Everlasting*.
How long will we be stuck here between
There's nowhere to go and *I'm dying*?

A BED FOR THE BURNED

That the air might, as you sleep on the anti-gravity bed,
peel. *Pellicula.* All those little pads on your back are feet. Take their legs
and crawl past this heat. Unrash the day. So that no one point is skin.
Pipe this pressure the cold words avoid. *These are the entries:*
whatever straw you are tending. The spine inside the extendable blue
sip. *Listen*, back and forth, are we growing or breaking?
The sound is the same crunch.

CHOKE

Silence by silence, the dissolve.
You have not come equipped for the clasp.
She wraps her hands around your neck
and waits for the melt to rasp. A stone
where it should be soft, uncleft.
The nurse tosses the unspeakable.
My hand strikes the petri, petrified.
We worried all our lives unreasonable.
Grandma swears we should chew everything,
even words, even tea. The problem is the stuffed
face in general. What are we to do with this
held breath, blue swell, the bloom
in the hardened pellicle? I can still feel it
on my hand, where you are drowning
on just a trickle.

RUSH-WICK

From stair to star, the *i* is drifting.
Up the banister, your pewter rings slip.
Sky a sculpture of ash. You point to the knotted
cord that lashes the pain in your only
chest. There's a fountain. An arc where the needle
flicks. I touch the cold end of the central
line. The axis we will take when the day wraps,
unwraps us. Mercury. Funiculus. There's a tug
on the quicksilver. Of the heart,
there is said to be, a little rope inside.

SPINY OAKWORM

As if the caterpillar chewing could be discerned from the pencil's scritch.

What we made, we made in our
dreams beside the jawing that went on

in glass jars, spinneret transcriptions
stiffening the air.

I dreamed of wool, raw
and uncorded. The hair that fell
around your bed.

.

When we wanted to change, we stripped in front of a three-way mirror
and turned slowly, slowly, one side peeling from the other.

.

Under a septic moon, the dock a planed
surface, all our lives stretched
beneath us. The story

of your father risking the Grand Beach
channel, your thin arms hooked around his held breath.

.

Today, the haunt of an ending that never happened:
our inflatable boat flipping out into the lake-
crease as I swim swim out to nothing more than my sealed

mouth. We watch it
to the end, the struggle
of the yellow moth peeling up
a lake, an old skin
snapping.

.

I was swimming and thinking about the swimming poem,
the one with the moth when

open and pale
as a palm, an oakworm flapped
the surface before me

a furred finger curling.

I carried it to the shore and laid it to dry
on my page. A wing darkening a word.

They take the same breath, the poem, the dying.
But the poem comes back.

.

Pain migrates the hand, the finer bones, the wrist.
Where we have held on to each other, let.

In the hospital, I scratched your legs until just before
bleeding. Or ecstasy.

With a calming effect, as an infant to the chest,
the oakworm crawls up my hand, leads.

I swim to feel my larger body.

.

If my father had let go, if his –

When we paddled out onto the glass
shelf of our childhood lake in the light

of sliced young fruit. A child so vividly
private, you, all thought hatched

inward. The opposite of ripple,
this movement.

AUCTION ITEMS

The day they pulled his body from the lake we became unafraid of snakes.

The aquarium sat in the rain as his red face narrowed through sand.

A man in dress pants walked out into the lake, let the waves unroll his cuffs.

There was nothing to hold onto. A canoe anchored to its own abandonment – two ends horning up from a submerged hull, rocking.

When she held up the snake, its body locked a stiff rope. End to end muscle clung to nothing but itself.

The auctioneer was late to the stage. He had been walking vigil through the night mumbling prayers fast as numbers.

There is a responsibility not to look at the grieving, but to witness the cloud that parts for the twelve gold bars pillaring the lake.

The auctioneer knows what we want to pay for, raises us gently with figures we understand.

It takes twenty-four hours for his body to surface. The family has requested we not know his name.

Everywhere "action" appears where "auction" should be.

The red canoe is the prize item we pretend not to want.

With numbers stuck to our chests.

"A reminder you must register your name before you can bid."

A wall hangs from the inflated vest.

More people than you think do not know how to swim.

That the snake can float its entire body upon the hook of her thumb.

It's the foreignness of such grasping, such taut air, not the snake, we fear.

The evening lake slips its skin, a sky, blue-grey, at our feet.

"Who will give me five dollars, five dollars for the snake, come on now, let's keep this alive here folks, don't let me give this away, five dollars for a forty dollar aquarium and a bonus snake…."

There is a moment the auctioneer is abandoned, when the bidders make their deals direct, one on one, above the crowd.

There are no faces, only hands, hands in the air, waving and just like that a bidder clasps his chest and bows out.

He was found ten feet below his boat twenty-four hours later with forty people on the shore. Candles, waxed saucers, and no moon streaked their faces.

The auctioneer didn't know the grandmother had placed a minimum fifty-dollar bid. So everyone lost and the cold-blooded moved inside.

One man who wanted to swim out in the night feels for him somewhere just below the imagination.

The rain was a blessing that afternoon – no child shrieking or swimming.

A pause came over the bidders when they opened their black umbrellas.

We came for a walk on the beach, forgetting. Stepped over the lines in the sand, the dragged rib of his boat.

No one marks the hours it takes for the wind to shift.

Everything on this edge has gone soft. The beerbottle, the divers.

At some point you must stop and think about what you are willing to carry away.

"Going once, going twice…"

This is the moment you get what you came for.

A show of hands tolling the air.

LARVÆ

[L. *larvæ:* a ghost, spectre, hobgoblin; also, a mask.]

Chrysalis, tell me your secrets.
When all our faces are cast, backlit,
what pushes through sun?

In this room, at this window, with a dry shake.
We wore sunglasses indoors, peeled moths
from the EXIT. Night was full
of soft sounds: wet paper, fuschias
waxing, and a tongue

pushed through. You spoke with two fingers
pressed to the chalaza. Not a word,
but a cord. The hinge on the inner
vibration. We all were.

VERNIX CASEOSÆ

That *fog* follows *foetus* in the dictionary.
Our first skin is light. Encased at the base

of every seed, a cere, old beak held to its
face. Let me show you the glairy

field where darkness becomes beam.
Where the grebe rolls in on its airy

cot. Spirit, make your imperfect
representation, your dim bodying

forth. (The blonde swatch
after 33 years still curls in the damp.)

To cast off:
Exuviæ.

Light split is still
light –

even our eyelids are peeling.

TRACHEOSTOMY

For your 33rd birthday we burn all the leaves.
Watch the air crumple the blanks in your eye.
That there are ways to gauge a cloud emptying,
but not this, the radius of a breath. I've heard
in a pinch the incision can be made with a *Bic*.
We are trying to imagine the length you will need
to write a word without yanking out the tube.
I think of the Unknown Comic's paper mouth.
Voice delivered from a slit. The remarkable sadness
at the kindergarten door waving with strings
tied to our wrists. Is this hope now?
The nurse calls them *ribbons* instead of *restraints*.
When I read *vitals* all I see are *vials* with a cross inside.

BALD-FACED

Vespa, paper: home with the sewn-up eyes: home with the open
mouth. *Listen:* the nest is chewing out an ear, the page on its way
to the soft consonant. Heart, is that you, dug up to your gums?
We have been sleeping for so long the night has rearranged
its teeth. Emptiness, you have far more body than I
imagined. What is breath but the parceled, celled interiors. The thin-
coiled rheostatics of swarm? Voice begins in the hum on a stick,
each molar fine-grinding the cold salt of Wonder
Bread and macaroni bologna. The dentist hands over my mouth
in a paper bag. I wonder if the page is anything more than a sewn-up
gasp. Did you hear the air collapse when plastic was discovered?
When we couldn't put our heads inside? I carry my mouth home
at my hip. It sits in my office under *"ideas for poems."* I am thinking
about construction. How speaking is its own joint. I see it right
there in the Dixie Cup that holds my grandmother's overbite.
The dentist suggests a nightguard. There's a clench in the air.

NEST

Mouth-wisp. That shred
of dangled

breath. Decay, limp decoy.

How there was nothing and now
a hum –

SECTION III · SWARM

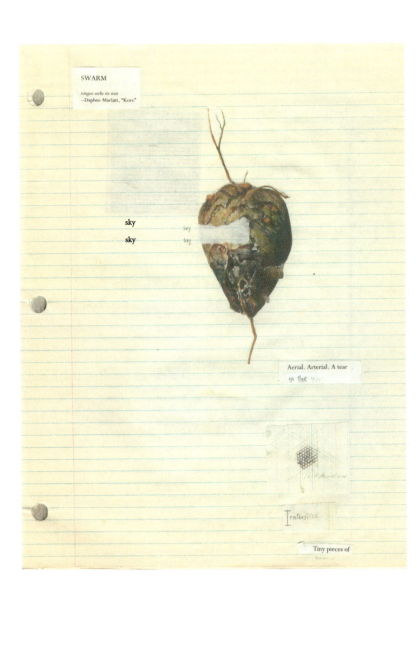

SWARM

tongue seeks its nest
--Daphne Marlatt, "Kore"

sky sky
sky sky

Aerial. Arterial. A tear
in the

Interstice

Tiny pieces of

HUM.

   hummen, sum-

      men,

          light;

      to

         mouth; to

    bees any

     low,

       applause;

            – *interj.*

      a pause,   *doubt*

     ahem. –

      murmur

          given to the in-

   sound

         A hollow
       which, when spun, emits

H
–
e
–
A
–

r,

t;   shred

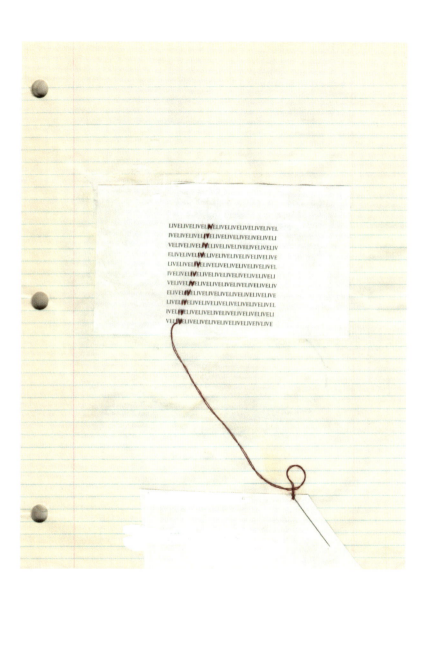

LA

rapid　　　　　pulp To make a stem, from
　　　　a　　　　　　　ornets and
asps are horizontal, and have　　　cell
side, each　　　　la　　) This central　, which
　　　　　　　　　　　　　with a pro
elope of layers of　　　　　　light　　open
the　　from. The　　is soon　　　　a multistoried
　　　　　　　　　z
olumnar support,
ally　the interior
bald faced　art
　　　　　　　　　　, a single
　　　　　　　　　　　　ils of their ne
　　　　　　　　　　ray　　　　　he hornets tend to
　　　their wood　　　　　　　　faces of telephone

　　　　　　　　　the source　　　　　' pulp
　　　　　　　Beam for
　　　　　　a kind of paper.

Papier-mâché

Even the abandoned have
weight. To be that
weathered fencepost spit
back as face,. I hang
on my central hum. Comb
saliva for cohesion.

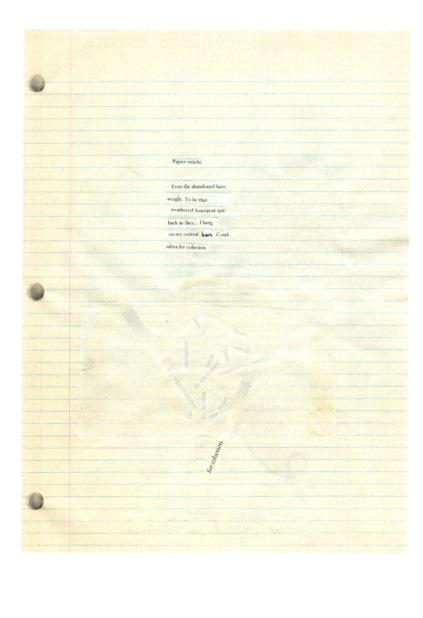

the morph in these blinks
Cake smallest points.
I dream through the am swim to. warmth
Arcadys. In these bright lines.
A hole through. Dilate.
There is no sight. are capped
in the yep the arm swims to the no page.
Reverie. Rest. Plunging. bleeds
There's a nest inside.
when the hand stops it I
hole
jitter.

ne t

PAPER   the common
                pain
        chews   hung
                              lo food is placed in
            egg
           The bald
     oval,
       0
drone   workers or
queens,   ion on the food eaten   e in
brood   ly spring   ich are
close   some under
and, some hidden   or under logs. An

                                            work 0.6"

line.   "A hole through."

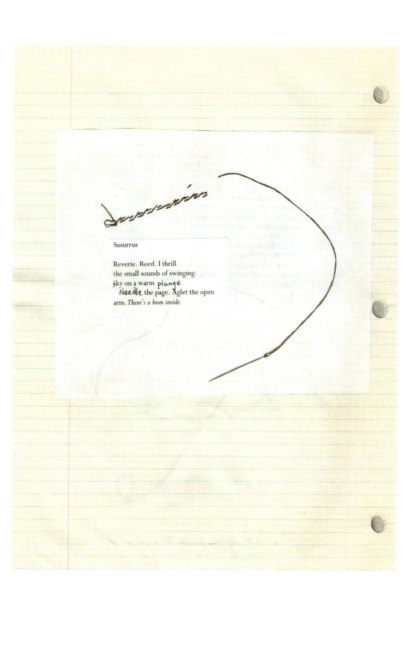

Susurrus

Reverie. Reed. I thrill
the small sounds of swinging
sky on a warm plunge.
Needle the page. Aglet the open
arm. *There's a hum inside.*

ULTRASOUND

This is how the heart should swim, with its entire gap.   Of airbladders, isinglass, *glue made from sounds.* Of survival. The old beam filling in the face. For cadence, interference, *see: decibels snowing.* For form, *see: a heart mouthing the static.*

Start again. *I hear you.*
Reception like a snake
in the grass. Mom's *s*'s
when she sings in the car.
A minute crushing
forward. All our silences go
kissing. They say hearing
is sharpest at birth and death
and once, before fainting, a dove
flew out of my ear. *Find your heart*
was the advice and all I heard was
a click. Long ago
my belief cracked. Not a hole
but a mild prolapse. Panic dives.
You won't even feel it. The line
tapering. The beaked air. *Tap gently*
she said: *home unwinds from the mouth.*

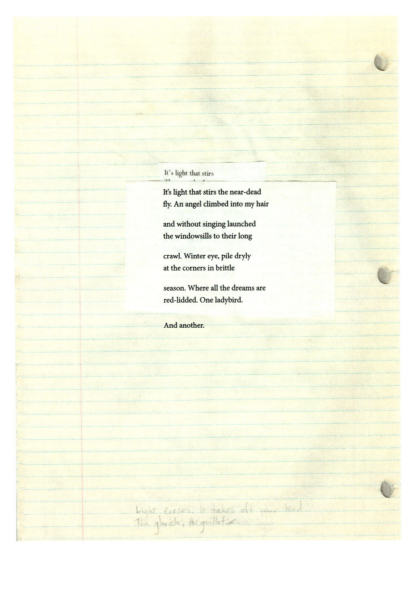

It's light that stirs the near-dead
fly. An angel climbed into my hair

and without singing launched
the windowsills to their long

crawl. Winter eye, pile dryly
at the corners in brittle

season. Where all the dreams are
red-lidded. One ladybird.

And another.

Light erases. It takes off your head.
The glovich; the guillotine

Cord

Insert cut.
A graphic scent.
The heart freshly tapped
to a new star. Beading. Hyaline
    Veins like windows.
We have been for so long
young. I stand at the broken
glass. A chrysalis scratches
    your eye. A drip pulls
back to its storm.

    this is how you dream:
with a vein open and a window
blown and the whole silent
frame filling.

The seed tasted like paper.

HEART SOUNDS

S₁

LUB

nub the
poem
rubs

S₂

DUB

bud
the bird
thumbs

lilium

hilum,
hum   where **breath**   root*s*
                              the lung   vague nerve ache

—*Apex*   in the upper branches

        (nest
                                            uppermost
—*Oblique* *flower*   the heart projects

        auricle,   whorl

                lodge   the   notch

SECTION IV · PAPERY ACTS

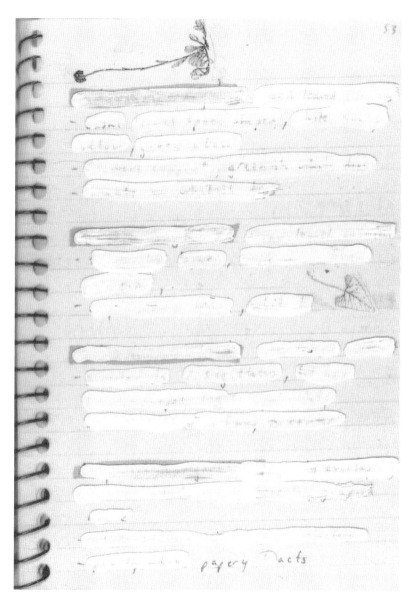

The poet of the hand dreams with his pencil upon the blank.
Gaston Bachelard

essay, v. [refashioned form of 'assay' after Fr. *essayer*]: to try by touch, to feel by handling.

Here, on the parchment scroll, I press my finger to the word and lift it. Read it reverse on my skin. I've shredded an entire manuscript, line by line, and am arranging it backwards on the tallest page I can find.

P. K. Page said she wrote poems to "follow a thread back." To search for something she already knew but had forgotten she knew. "To listen – not to but for." I cut up my poems to hear what I'm trying to say.

"Poetry is long," Tim Lilburn said to me 20 years ago. I think I'm beginning to understand.

I compose with my hands. Meaning pencil, longhand. I think first through movement – doodling, stitching, clipping – the feel is my guide.

"You can't separate what I'm saying from the actual form in which it's said," says Margaret Atwood.

I can't separate the poem from my hand.

Poem comes from the Latin *to make*.

I'm shifting away from *writing* poems to *making* them.

.

I work with scraps, shreds, fragments. A scroll is a type of scrap. From the Anglo French *escrowe*: a screed, a parchment, a strip.

Working with scraps – pieces of narrative, mine and others – I'm listening for where the poem and life crossover. I'm looping, stitching, hooking words into some kind of poetry net.

Scrap, from *scrapa, scrape*: "to erase." I'm learning that the entire effort can be turned around. That the poem, like a field, when leveled, can regenerate.

"To erase," says Jeannie Vanasco, "is to leave something else behind."

.

It was a long silence that brought me to the erasure poem. Not mine, but my brother's, during his many months in a coma.

I came across a notebook of his – a pocket-sized, handwritten field guide of prairie grasses. I read it for companionship, signs of consciousness, attention. I read it for the rhythms of his still and distant hand.

Here, in my brother's small and steady print were the words for the smallest botanies, the most hidden plant structures: *awn, lemma, glume.* The tufts of hair at the end of a seed.

Written in Latin, their meanings escaped me. So I read for texture, association, rhythm, opening. I read for motion, life, the raw breath of my brother's long dream. After a while the words seemed to stand up, backlit with glorioles, dandelion pappi. They came at me new, ghosted: *awe, dilemma, gloom.*

In this field, the vast page between my brother's silence and my vigil ear, a voice balanced on a tuft of grass; a seedpod dragged up a whole field behind it: *silique* drifted into *soliloquy.*

.

In her long erasure poem, *Little White Shadow,* Mary Ruefle composes with Wite-Out, creating meaning through disappearance. "The only way I can describe it is like this," Ruefle says, "the words rise above the page, by say an eighth of an inch, and hover there in space, singly and unconnected, and they form a kind of field, and from this field I pick my words as if they were flowers."

.

Brooklyn poet and visual artist Jen Bervin constructed her long poem "*The Desert*" by sewing row by row, line by line, across 130 pages of John Van Dyke's, *The Desert: Further Studies in Natural Appearances* (1901). Bervin's drafts, all 30 of them, were constructed exclusively by following the pale blue zigzag stitch over the page. The result is a poem "narrated by the air, so clear that one can see the breaks."

.

Intention. I'm trying to shake her. But I can't take *the me* out of *theme*. All dressed up in ambition, I hear her every time: the dead line in the deadline. What was once cadence is now Candace, the tallest girl in the school at free period leading me around by the back of my neck with a squeeze. I pretend it doesn't hurt. Refuse to flinch. But she is on me and I am adapting my swallow to the pinch. There is a point when my every move accommodates her hold. When my silence protects her grip.

.

I confess, when I first read a poem I hear only breath. Isn't it true that 90% of what we communicate is nonverbal? *Meaning can be so distracting.*

The word is only the mule the breath rides in on. Listen: above and below the line: the iamb's tender hoof. *For so long, all we had was his breath.*

.

There's a man with prosthetic eyes that walks without a cane or guide dog. He feels his way through space by clicking his tongue. It's like echolocation – the clicks bounce off objects in the environment and he moves around them. Guided by his own reverberation. These are the first sounds I trust in a poem. Breaths and clicks.

.

Hyoid bone, tongue bone, the only bone in the human body that floats. It is a small anchor there in the throat named after the upsilon, the Greek letter *u* meaning *rough breath*.

For so long it was all we had – my brother's breath. A white flare in the tube: cocoon, fog patch, misty field.

Silence piles atop silence.

Hyoid follows *hymn* in the dictionary. And *hum*. There's a twig inside the hornet's nest, floating. I hold up the swarm, let out its beam. A sonogram wings for the face. There's a picture in that field I can't yet see.

Move in with your hum.

.

My most recent composition is a collage of words taken from my grandmother's 1950s Roger Tory Peterson field guide *How to Know the Birds*. I have only half the book. Pages 94–168. *To Know* sits here on my desk, lopped off its spine.

The scrap poem is about impermanence. Transformation. A book falling apart can be a wondrous thing. Meaning takes a whole new direction. "There are many pleasures in tearing apart one's own publications," says Phil Hall. "In this way – the artifact re-experiences woe … let the woe flow through the artifacts."

Grief Silhouettes, this book I collaged out of the broken one: Already the glue has dried, the words are drifting.

·

The smallest and perhaps most whimsical and innovative elements of Emily Dickinson's writings – her "variant marks," have been mostly dismissed by editors and publishers. The Dickinson poems we read are the polished, dusted, trim versions. Recent efforts have sought to correct this – *The Gorgeous Nothings* by Granary Books is a reproduction of her envelope writings – the original writings have been reproduced along with typographical representations. Not only her variant markings, but her handwriting has been represented. These once hidden and now exposed originals help us to reconsider the relationship between a poem and the scene of its initial creation; they encourage us to re-think our assumptions about what constitutes a 'finished' poem.

·

The Finished Work. I have come to be stymied by The Finished Work. Oh great certainty! Oh great pretend! Words shouldn't act as if they know something (you know those words). They scare me into silence.

"In poetry," says Gaston Bachelard, "non-knowing is a primal condition; if there exists a skill in the writing of poetry, it is in the minor task of associating images."

Mary Ruefle: "Deprivation is desire. Isolation is lust."

·

Recently, an attention and a fascination with the shapes of things. Their silhouette. Their ombromonie. A grebe in the fog can be a floating question mark. A hand, at the right angle, a beak.

Poetry as a type of shapemaking, becoming. The outlines point to the inlines.

The glue dries, the words fall, the poem is alive again, shifting. *Chance*, taking its small hook, becomes *change*.

.

My first writings were epistolary. I was 10-years-old writing to an invented self I called "Superstitious Me." Each letter was handwritten on my mother's finest stationary, slipped discretely from the top drawer of her rattly china cabinet. It was the time in childhood when everything felt urgent, secretive, possible. It felt powerful and naughty to write in a secret voice to a secret self. I sealed the letters and dropped them unaddressed in the mailbox at the end of our street. Not long after, the mailbox had to be exterminated – a swarm of bees had taken it for a hive. I imagined my letters behind it all. Each envelope split into a honeycomb. My words worked by bee legs, rearranged into hexagons. Meaning crawling back into its sticky cell. Everything I have written since has been listening for the low drone of those first letters. Every poem has been trying for their sealed hum.

.

"We need to find our own way to take this place into our mouth; we must re-say our past in such a way that it will gather us here." (Tim Lilburn)

The stitched poem, the built poem, is my attempt to find a surprising way of working that I don't question.

Jen Bervin runs a page under the pressure-foot. She moves forward. Only forward. Like breath. She can't delete.

"The poet is goosed along by an intuitive something." (Dennis Lee)

·

That summer the fog scrolled over me as I wrote on the dock and my brother slept long under a thin white sheet. The grebe moved in and out, a question mark.

These are all just scrap thoughts. Shadows behind the curtain, working to save my brother, my poem. My hand over the page grows a beak.

Jeannie Vanasco: "To erase is to leave something else behind."

·

Let's just say it: Words – you scare me: *a fraud* is just one stroke away from *afraid*.

When my daughter is afraid I tell her: *Put silly putty in your pocket and pinch.*

When I'm afraid I think of poet Anne Szumigalski's chicken angels in the trees, waving down to me with their cold & rosy hands.

·

When Anne Szumigalski got glasses at age five she grieved the loss of her father's "magic Christmas lights": "I would never be bamboozled by such things again. I would see things as they really are, or at least as everybody else saw them."

·

"Life is the greatest thing that ever happened to me," says my daughter.

"To exist is the artist's greatest pride. [She] desires no paradise other than being," says Osip Mandelstam whose poems often began physically, as a ringing in the ears. A process he described as "the recollection of something that has never before been said." He didn't sit at a desk, but rather paced, walked through the streets, muttering until he was lost, his lips moving while he walked.

.

The question, always: *how to record the breath?* The weave, the wave, the ripple where the grief dives.

.

I remember liking everything I read. I actually did. I liked everything. I didn't know what I didn't like. But I knew what I liked *more*.

.

Stammer. Waver. The poem of repair. Away from the machine I go. From the curser's monotonous cut.

There's a tone, a slope in handwriting that you can't get in typeface. A thread-like wiggle.

Larvae, that silent little cruncher, it means "mask." Handwriting, it crawls around, nibbling.

.

The idea every poem has its extreme object form. A wordlessness, a wildness. A secret shape. My true marker of having exhausted or created a poem is when I can imagine its material form, its fullest, barest, embodied silence.

•

In 2001, I was part of a small group of poets and artists to found JackPine Press, a limited-edition chapbook publisher who challenges the notions of what a book can be. The writers and designers of each book have full creative control of every aspect of their work, from what it says to how it opens and turns or doesn't. Many of the JackPine chapbooks employ a sense of chance/participation from their reader, opening in many ways, in various directions.

Between 1858 and 1864 Emily Dickinson grouped her poems into small hand-bound packets, later called fascicles. They were humble bindings: stab-bound with twisted red and white thread.

Rebecca Solnit: "I still think the revolution is to make the world safe for poetry, meandering, for the frail and vulnerable, the rare and obscure, the impractical and local and small."

•

I made a chapbook of my childhood home wrapped with inverted 1970's couch upholstery and vinyl floral wallpaper. The title *nest* is stitched with my mother's scrap yellow yarn from the baby sweater she was knitting for me while she was pregnant. The sweater remains just a back and a sleeve, half-finished. The book is concertina, bound only by folds. It goes around and around, never ending.

•

Jules Michelet in Gaston Bachelard's essay on "Nests":

"The form of the nest is commanded by the inside … the instrument that prescribes a circular form is nothing else but the body of the bird. It is constantly turning round and round and pressing back the walls on every side.

The house is a bird's very person; it is its form and its immediate effort, I shall even say its suffering. The result is only obtained by constantly repeated pressure of the breast. Surely with difficulty in breathing, perhaps even with palpitations…."

.

A page under the pressure foot, a stab-bound bundle. The poem as architecture. A home we live inside. Maybe it's the pressure of these little books, their labour (the books are produced in editions of 75), but there's something bodily about the chapbook. I was a few weeks pregnant when I made mine and I still feel nauseous when I open it.

.

I think of Emily Dickinson building her books, her fascicles. Lowering her handwritten notes in a dumbwaiter down to the neighbourhood kids. Not a shut-in artist, but a playful spirit, gathering and engaging with the world privately, gently.

Emily was a botanist. She collected grasses and flowers, some she pressed with her poems. *Fascicle*, meaning bunch or bundle, is also a botanical term, for a clustered tuft of leaves, flowers. She had a customized pocket sewn into her dress for her pencil and notebook. "Poetry is a response," says Roo Borson. "Compact and light, it is a traveller's art form."

.

The scrap poem, Emily's envelope writings. Her – 's and + 's.

Jen Bervin layered and embroidered these previously hidden and ignored marks of Emily's, large-scale, on cotton batting with red thread. "I wanted to see what patterns formed when all of the marks in a single fascicle, remained in position, isolated from the text, and were layered in one composite field of marks."

Not indecision, as these marks have been called, but rather seed-scatter, constellation, brachial branching.

.

I am listening for where the poem and life crossover. *The letter with the hive with the hum.*

"Open, I say. She is mindfully open. A dreamer. A quiet wide-awake child writing a letter to an imaginary friend." (C.D. Wright)

.

My brother, when he's out of the hospital, says to me: "The biomass of the soil is what makes the forest thrive. There's so much going on underground that we can't see."

Erasure as regeneration. Silent stammer. A growing *under*.

My brother's illness was a constant process of breakdown and regeneration. Under his long sleep, the physiology that took place inside his body was almost unthinkable. A re-building of the skin. The nail. The eyelid. The voice.

In a chrysalis, the larvae digests itself down to a few imaginal discs. So that literally the entire contents of the caterpillar – the muscles, the digestive system, the heart, even the nervous system – are totally rebuilt. There is a disc like a seed floating in the chrysalis from which each organ will sprout: The heart. The eye. The leg. The antennae.

Bachelard: "The poem is a continuous passage from the real to the imaginary."

When my brother wakes up, his face has slipped. Dream has a different gravity.

"The page enacts a transformation," says Phil Hall.

We are built on our daily movements, however small, unconscious. The muscle it takes to swallow. To blink.

•

It took me seven years to realize every time I wrote *end* in my poem I really meant *begin*.

Bachelard: "The instinctive human supposition that any word may mean its opposite."

•

The cells in the human body, except the cerebral cortex, are said to regenerate every seven years.

The poem is most often inside-out. "The sentence kind of turns back on itself," says Lynne Tillman. "The tail eats the head."

•

To bypass intention. Allow for new order. I call it backcombing the poem. Going against the setting to create a kind of detailed, grainy fray. The halo of a shredded strand. *A tuft of grain at the end of seed*. In flipping the poem, I am trying to find its health, its transformation. "On the other side of horror," says Rilke, "is something helpless that wants help from us."

•

When a snake sheds its skin does it crawl out as if slipping through a tunnel or does the skin fold off, invert like a sock?

•

Lyn Hejinian: "Every mark on the paper is an insertion into a kind of peace."

Phil Hall's ragged left margin. A ripple there, staggering the rule.

Mark Goldstein's word-bleeds, like Bervin's layered fascicles, shining through. Pages turned transparent in his *Form of Forms*.

To break down and reconfigure. *The page enacts a transformation.*

•

When I was 12, I used to erase my hands. I wanted them to be different than they were – smoother, younger, plumper than the bony "old-soul" grandma hands I was born with. I used the cosmetic "cover-up" the way one would try to smooth a face. *I can't separate the poem from my hand.* When I was 12, I erased my voice.

•

"Every child who shuts himself in desires imaginary life," says Bachelard. "It seems that the smaller the retreat in which the dreamer confines himself, the greater the dreams."

"The most enclosed being creates waves." (Yanette Deletang-Tardiff)

•

I came across a book of poetry by Wave Books with back cover copy that was slightly bent. Not the page, but the line. It was designed with a wrinkle in it, a refraction. A crimp jumped up through meaning.

·

I look to materials that capture and hinge and unwind: thread, vintage field guides, fonts, pigments, cyanotype, thread spools, licorice lace, film reels, photocopies, handwriting, honeycomb bells, hinging tape.

·

It's the sound of unwinding I want. Fifty thousand red-sided garter snakes emerging from their hibernaculum in the spring. The high sound of leaves scraped low. Some believe snakes navigate by star.

Dennis Lee: "A poem thinks by the way it moves."

·

There's something honest and raw and intimate about the handmade that I want my writing to embody. I believe if I'm working physically close to the text that this closeness, this lean, might also be somehow *read*.

·

I wind the scroll around the room. A white lining on the walls. One end goes on to meet the other. *Harking back as if history were something carried forward or cyclic with a twist in the end.* A fog drifts off the bay. A tuft of hair under your bed collects. Breath in the tube. A cocoon. *Poetry … the minor task of associating images.*

·

Breath, child's breath, stretched inside car windows. Touch by touch we burn through. Connect. Where the finger lifts, a droplet, a star.

·

How to see the marks themselves as points of transformation. Naftali Bacharach's picture poem, "Poem for the Sefirot as a Wheel of Light," *sefirot* meaning *emanation*. The sefirot serifing their whipped flame tips.

·

It's a long skin, what I find in the gravel of the parking lot. It includes the skin of the eye. The nictitating third inner lid.

A tunnel, a cave, the scroll is a spool winding/unwinding. Bi-directional. Roy Kiyooka: The long poem is "what moves me most, serpent-wise, through the body of my speech."

Don McKay: "Poems can get pulled out like tape measures and/or fishing line.

·

Stitching, because it's what I want words to do. Pick a definite point and move finely through.
·

I use books to bookmark books: Spines within spines: *The Golden Guide to Birds* inside *Thinking & Singing* inside *The Right to Dream*. Feather-ruffle.

·

These are spatial compositions. Atmospheres of change and chance. A knot blots out a letter. Hesitation, that worm, stretches the line. The hand, so close to the page, is recorded there: my pulse alters a word.

"Hey Jenn" my husband calls out "*and* is going down the drain!" See, the poem follows you. The line loosens. Margins tug and drift.

.

"To imagine is to absent oneself," says Bachelard. "It is a leap toward a new life."

.

When you sleep, the edges of your breath sound like a pencil sharpening. Dennis Lee says all poetry is first scribbling.

The pen is a beak: peck peck peck.
Words! Such little scratches at the feeder!

.

I'm interested most in the page as transitory, regenerating. Shed surfaces. Impermanence. Bi-directional texts that can be read both ways. Altering.

Scrolls were the first form of editable record keeping texts, used in ancient Egyptian civilizations. The ink used in writing scrolls had to adhere to a surface that was rolled and unrolled, so special inks were developed. Even so, ink would slowly flake off. Meaning sifted. Words fell. If the ink from too many letters is lost, a Torah scroll is no longer used.

.

When I stitch and cut and erase poems I am asking for something more. Something *extempore*, out of time, imrovisatory, unexpected. I don't just want to *write* a poem, I want to *encounter* it.

.

"Steer by the ear," says Lee. Listen for the space we hadn't known before: the click in the mouth, the setback house, *soliloquy* in the seedpod.

I could see the machine punching the frozen ground but each time the sound arrived just after the action.

Kroetsch's poetics of delay: silence slipped between the ear and the eye. Let's treat the page as acoustic space. Taut drum. "I wanted to fill every silence with a word and every word with a silence." (Dionne Brand)

.

My great grandmother cross-stitched flowers and birds. She followed a pattern, along a screened grid knowing just where she was going. She knew what it would look like, where she would end up, and yet still she kept going.

Pleasure there, just there, in the moment of the draw, colour filling in. Simple progress, thread by thread.

I feel none of that as a writer. But I want to. There is no progress, just endurance. When we look back, a wider hole.

.

My mom teaches me to change my grandmother's earguard. Hands over the tiniest screw. Inside the pink pointer (the inner ear looks like a finger) I thread, unthread a sound.

.

When we work with our hands, we are listening tangibly to a space. A thread pulled over a word encourages a new sound, a new meeting of marks. The page reads not just its words, but its entire atmosphere.

"What the poem mimes," says Lee, "is not a static structure, but an active cohering."

.

I am watching what fills in when I clip a word from a page. What pools up from below.

She caught me in the field looking for a skin. "You're acting out the poem," she said. I didn't know how else to find it.

.

I look at the stitches now and see evidence of her hand in motion. I flip it over to the stops and starts – tiny knots tied off at intervals.

The inversion gives me hope. That the broken can be turned around. That the turning can make things new.

I take up the afghan, all her movements wrap my body. I take up the scroll.

.

The scrap poem as suture. A mend. The scrap poem as prayer. Amen.
"The acts of rhythmic attention are a species of natural prayer."
(Dennis Lee)

If the act is what we praise. If we subscribe to a prayer of *doing*.

The poem is animate: *filled with breath*.

"To live consciously is holy." (Gwendolyn MacEwan)

The poem is animate: *A current of wind, the vital principal*: *to rouse*.

I leave my mark. Above that, something hot off the breath. "The poem, a broken whisper" (Ruefle).

Look: there is *praise* in *respiration. Repair.*

·

I push words around until they say something. I break language until I hear my most buried voice. When Alice looks back, the hole is closed. Mary Ruefle: "I remember the first time I realized the world we are born into is not the one we leave."

·

Poets, we are labourers. We move words, dusts. Carve out a little bit of sound. Shift it back and forth. Turn the hourglass. *Poetry is the result of a conflicting impulse to connect and hide.*

·

Lyn Hejinian: "Writing's initial situation, its point of origin, is often characterized and always complicated by opposing impulses in the writer that language cannot resolve. The writer experiences a conflict between a desire to satisfy a demand for boundedness, for containment and coherence, and a simultaneous desire for free, unhampered access to the world."

·

I didn't come to poetry knowing or writing. I came digging, with puttied hands.

SECTION V · THORN

As to what to grow? Ah, that is the question, gardener grow

your will

will

will

Page 48

Filling Gaps in Old ▓▓ Beds

Countless disappointments have been
caused by
an established bed

a hole is not
a garden,

To successfully grow   the heart
       take pains to understand
                   this queen of

          readiness
        upon a sunny
         spade

            prune a rose

Showing where to prune

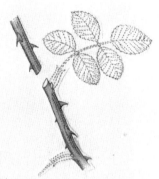

    middle state

    for many years
    "rose-sick"

        hardly visible to the dormant eye   a
                                    sharp
                                    tear

                    in a bucket

    Empty space
    is vital   the location of the
  cut in relation to the
  numb

the sun gets stronger

in
a wine glass of kerosene

crown.

the balanced head
       cut off.

       Glory Radi-
       ance   admit sunlight and air.

from a ringlike mark consider
   the point of lead in a pencil, pruned back
       to the base
   The most common error made
   in formal beds is
       a long record of
            perfect
   yellow- and pink-tinted Peace.

HEDGE

Hereditary, hederaceous, hourglass –

The line grows into itself.
Trying for the widest possible

privacy – a chin hair, lawn-chair, under-the-knee sting
follicle. H*ag,* caragana, *haga* urticaria.

A single rogue gray
trespasses the profile.

Of *acus, aculeus,* the acute follow.
Of *hairs, hours* crossed.

Exchange *life* for *line* in any instance.
Property for *poetry.*

Our lot: a bristle
of funneled sands.

.

Heirloom

Hair, they say, *hair of leaves is sharper than a needle.*
The hourglass grows its thorn.

Submerged, our heartbeat scrubs, our heartbeat
with a wooden handle knocks the wall. *Tock tock.*

Spade. Bloody shovel. *Not meaning to – this far –*
Put any two words together and let them arc.

The button you pressed said *Lifeline*.
Cuts, they have their own mouths.

Flower Clock   *In height, to some extent*

To drift the boundary, widen the hour: snow.
Eigenlicht, own light, on your face, eternity.

"The sky is white, the ground is white, are we upside down?"
Turning and turning the difference

between press and draw,
in the needle, the hourglass.

Time as bloom: *3 am Goat's Beard, 5 am Ox Tongue.*
Not brightness, but contrast. The eye searching

for horizontals, a place to live. Minutes, bulbets.
The garden advances. Longbacks through trees.

Crosshairs.

·

Arcminute

At what degree are we
in the lean of the constant

face. The entire fence
clacks down

when you open your mouth
to give up your teeth. Picket

by picket, the home
collapses, deciduous.

Paean for Peony

Rub the eyes with charcoal. Roots without eyes are worthless.
Forty-seven years of latent light. Light drawn down through a stem.

Oh root, perfumed shoulders. Oh worm, lightshy lips.
The palette is skin. Once, maybe twice, I will dig you back in.

Privet, picket

Lilac unclasps. Your mouth
on the window, an arranged breath

in full nightgown, nil panicle.
A blue stands up at the glass.

Nod and nod.
Bud. Capillary.

The back of your hand raises
its map. Scent has no gate

but memory. The hour peels
its paint. Petals

 – *eyelets, scissored bonnet* –

through and back, we go
through and back.

.

Transplant   inter

I carried you out with folded arms:
perfumed wrist, root vegetable, watercress.

I have never broken a bone but I have broken a line
badly. The bucket

shifts: garden bed, bottom chamber.

I misread *roof* as *root*.
The home is changing.

.

Sundial

Trying to make a loop of it, that we might not end
in the next line, where the hour floats.

Yes, there is an *I*, a gnomon holding its pen.
And a *you* paddling along as if we were quaint.

Let's pretend things are just as they are.
That the shadow grows into its next blue.

And no age owns us but the light and the snow
and the scrub oak holding out its scale.

I'm thinking of chimes now. Ice blown over ice.
A window. The almost-colour

of varied descent. Viridescent
hover, hummingbird

figure-eights, where flowers spring
just above the branch.

.

Quickset, deadset

Turn it over. Forty-one years of trying
for the honest line. To forage the foliage. The fallacy.

What if the poem wasn't about the poem? Would it have words?
                                                                      Kinds?

Reset the root,

the hour, a flower
unjawing.

SECTION VI · GRIEF SILHOUETTES

GRIEF SILHOUETTES

climb upwards into the
Mourning
    the
      never-ending
        turf

sparrows foretell the snows
all winter
the seed glean
through the bleak

.

Swallow   skims close to the
                    Blue   in late

                        Meadow
                        Pipits pass

        where cattle have chewed
            possession   hayfields

        Whistle   the Bald patch

                            .

                        heart
                            old Knot hole in the
                Orchard
                            chains rattled off
            Fly
                    by Fly

            there was health in spots

                            sun
                    between men killing   trees
                                            little-
                                            eyed

            you can see then   why the
            light is scant   an insect scourge

            thirty-three years old

                        chance dwells in every garden

.

        and they were spaced more openly
the numbers   air won over to boxes
    Chimney, the Cuckoo

    business skimmed the sky   broken Yellow
Warblers gave way to high buildings, growing
    shorter wings

believe
me, bi-level   edge
    is the point of transition

    the birds change too

                                     .

                        dry year

                        to crop
                        breath

                        when there is not enough

                        Song   balance axe on airway

                        moisture
                        drop first anchor

·

edge   to describe all borderline teenagers
Tanagers   hole-nesters   Crest cavities
        abandoned bottomland

where Ovenbirds chant
     (the Hooded
        Red-eyed Cerulean   range

competition among kin is keenest

    shade your habit

·

                            of all those
                            mentioned

                      edges
                         are lovers
                        of sunlight

·

      hem   home

        the border
        of higher
        states

     Flicker   Down and Hair

     a kind   Blue-headed   thrive

．

                  obligated to the
                  bogs,   live-sides
                  where usnea moss drapes the

               Throat   lack-
                                stunted

         cheek

．

     Blue
     day,
Night shift
     trill

          wiry

like a mouse with a tooth-ache

       rub

     Long
             the pitch

.

coo

reeds all over   swarm
                   pattern   epaulettes, gur-

  pump
                bubble   chorus

your lack list will soar

       rain
  skimming   your head

  wading about
a high   preserved
  per acre   (where once there had been

Rail, follow the   *-leeeeeee*

.

    here
   under
    the
    War

half-way down the

       page-
      mirror

in full view   my Hooded

      dabble
     ever
        difficult to

reed   the narrow strip
        the hidden

      Hero: Solitary
   Prothonotary Throat

              .

       this process goes on
         to *re-* the self
      go fallow, go Pheasant
allow the ills disturbed field, second-
    growth   time's spindly slash
     angle the hour to its ash
     the Mourning is not over

                                                    .

                                                    abundant
                                              Bunting

                                         tier
                                           the
                                                Blue

                                  abandoned

                  .

            ease brier
      Northern little brother
   it is hard to draw the line between

                     rafter
    and Vesper   prayed one

             pilfer the scratchfeed
                stick close to

                   the changing

.

describe bottomland
    Least Arctic
  respite estuaries

a motionless face-roster
artificial   Laughing reservoir
  have a bird

glass-
eyed
divers

billed
      in

lack   the Great
      lover

                              .

                endlessly   behind the vast   salt
              Throats gasp their ecological

                requirements

                        weak Song reside
                        on the next page

                            Egrets
                are met, invade the Swallow

.

to the lee   the life
that lies tucked
    raise your

  poison   a few

   Heroes can al-
   ways be found

.

               of stunted Throats
       and Song trees

        Flicker
        further
        Ipswich

    love
    the level stretches

     their sparse
     portrait

so some die　　　it is nature's way of opening up
　　the air　　　the long meeting place
　　　of us Common Pipers　　　there are always
　　　　　Lack and Gull　　　*head for*
　　　　the inlets, Little parties
　　　　if you wish to join them

　　　　　lovers, Knots and Semi-
　　　　migrations　　　of the outer
　　　　　heart travel the Least
　　　reaches where the remember
　　　　　　breaks through

　　　　　　　　　　　　　　Heroes
　　　　　　　　　　　　live along
　　　　　　　　　　no habit　　other than
　　　　　　　　　　　a good mud

.

    vantage
    an inlet where
    certain Grebes raft

      in a fishing boat you stand
a chance to dive beyond

          the self

    and in the ever-present earwater

        drift is some headland

                .

            tip point   rest

              behind
                    the cost
          of finding something

        less   Song –
        if you go out far –

        aches and flats
        scales on stiff wings

·

semipalmate the breast

prize
Puffin

duplicate Dovekie

alle alle

·

how many curses
per square praise Old Squaws,
Dowitchers, Curlew and

a host

the Lack-bellied
Red-backed
cold-climate within

valleys prevail

you will
change as you climb

·

    teeter along the margin, petrified
Petrel   flit in the wake of Auk

each change in art   is a change in the ache

see: *rare*   *(I'd like to*

                    with you

see: *chase*

      the finally
firs

           ·

      attraction
      in a few scant
      ports   swarm
      lines
          the near

  on
     and on
and

    the tide *ta-*
      migra-

         ropes swimming us out to

the ravel land

.

                count
        the near life   the average
        hours   these are the possible

            goods ma-
                jority White-rumps   Swallow

the
            condition

                                        .

                                kiss Dickcissel
                        rage and often far

                                the Broad-winged
                        alive in   drier woods

                        from the leafy floor your

                        Rose-breast Hood

.

    this little book is slanted
to an open spot in the
  thatch, the degree of longing
     in   the brown grass
that is transcontinental

     prefer wet feet   lily-clad brothers
          and the price
            of difference

                                .

                                life

                would you not have
                followed

                      holes   the same
                holes at the core
                of Orchards

           what beyond to boast
                on the page?

.

       trotter, poor
       tenant

       from an
       ornithological point of view

hearts start almost identical

      notice when you ascend

   the way
          the eaves course
            the storm

               .

              there is a
              woods   that   beaks
                        the edge of
       such found places, bird

              have a wet
              reach, and

    .

       for a full turn
       consult a Field

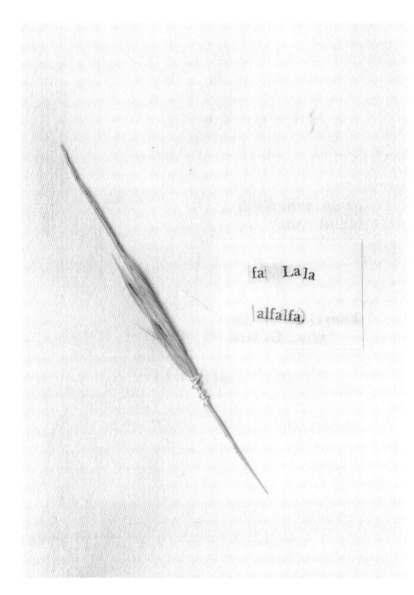

SECTION VII · COMMA

COMA

A coma is the blurred appearance of an object as seen under a microscope.
A tuft of hair at the end of a seed.

The full-stop, when magnified, is a meteor burning through all our meaning.
Every sentence ends with the 22 amino acids it takes to seed a planet.

A sundog is a coma, the broken halo of your mouth.
You smile 22° distant above the horizon.

The horizon is a highball. Your gloriole, your zero glyph.
We shoot you backlit, into the sun.

New fallen snow reflects 95 percent sunlight.
You drift out in moonboots, printing the sky.

A coma is a comma, the starfall of your hair.
I wait for you in the comb sounds.

MELIC, MELANCHOLILY

      limbsong;   lyric bile, black and *chole*,   holy

          char-
          gloom.   The great millet

          resembles leguminous
          humour.

                    The contents

            of clover,   lovers

                    honey
              honey

              hart's-song

INCUNABULA, NEBULA

                                                      once upon a swaddled
                prefix   there was an

          auri-

              CULA
              a whorl

and a FASCICLE, *fas'si-kl, n.*

                a little bundle of
                  lobed folia

      Bot. growing
            from

                the FASTEN.

                How to fix
                one's self
                      fascinate that air

      about you,
           petiole

               a spurred

          gold

STRAW STAR

lie down, down

stratus the scattered

      mouths,   limb home

                wing,   flapsheet

climb at the outer edge
of order

  as we sift   and
            bury

                a mothball with each
     courage.

        Corms

  inside baskets or boxes

 or eyes

    made of
      vertice,   barely

       below
  the
    ~~su~~rface

PALPEBRA, PAPPUS, PAPYRUS

write to me   pulse

Pulsatilla   P. patens.   all parts   resembling

bulbs

lift
foliage
catalogue

the
sunny
selves.

May lot
over a long

pleasure
form

CINNA LATFOLIA, ENDGRASS

Lit
    -ligule
    , edges rolled

  under red berries   *lax*   lingua   *acuminate*

a kiss on the prominent
papillose

                        pain is tall, inflorescent, nodding

pilose against pillows
millet, in soft shapes

WINTER ROSE, SPARSELY

I don't know densely the solitude
of the rosette spinning
on your finger

    Involucrate occidentalis

    memory's membraneous
    fluctuating –

        Alar, elixir

cell   where we are all rolled
      thread-like,
           toothless

              capsule, *calyptra*

        metrical, metrical
        may the marks we leave
        under mouth
        be

ACHE, ACHENE

Hyaline, hairline

                        a doe wanders in licking
                        the ciliate: ice lattices, eyelash

                        hairbirds in the rice
                        grass. Vibratile

                        witness,   the whiteness
                        the indehiscent hinge

CROCOSMIA X CROCOSMIIFLORA

breath-flare   winter ferns
    ahem   on the window   a clearing

in the cedar sedation   amnesiacs
                         long-bough
                                      icicles, auricles, the long-
stemmed

      stairfall, starwell
      careful not to stand too close to the

C-curled on the L-shaped   *hallucination.*

                    Northern-haired compass
                    needle toward

                            the blue day:
                            periwinkles

                            ion-spans
                            eyelash, axil

spiral
the sparse spines

SILIQUA, SOLILOQUY

tilde-field
serif-wicks

           ~ ~ ~ ~
           ~ ~ ~ ~

      a drift on your breath
      where you stagger

    the scandent

        pyxis
        an axis

    with a blackout
    over the engine:

                frozen lashes   match-heads
                sapdrops   chrysanthemum

                      a spark

                every time
                you blink

SPIRÆA, ASPIRATION

mauve beak   crocus,   your

downy

pith-
filled

oval

    a whisper in the
      ~~stomy~~ story

SYRINX, SYRINGA

Cannula, little reed
light sings light. Listen:
the lumen is whistling

CORYMB, CANDELABRA

We have come to carry the Golden Bean
trellice, *tell us*

        monkeyflower, spur   the urn-curved
        funnelforms

under this
frond parasol, in our masked half-

faces
    what we are

HAREBELL

        Your blue eye sheds
        a single black

                seed.   All it takes

is a fleck
on your cheek   one eyelash

                          rattled
                          from its lantern

                to hyphenate

                                – *a slit in the air that just goes*

                awn

      and awn

                        and awn –

            the dream

NOTES

COMMON BLUE was created in spring 2014 for friends and family as a handmade chapbook in an edition of 7. SCROLL was composed in fall 2014 on a 16-foot parchment scroll. SWARM was composed in fall 2014 in my mother's *Le Voyageur* exercise scribbler, single edition. PAPERY ACTS was created for the University of Winnipeg *Carol Shields' Writer-in-Residence Distinguished Lecture Series*, February 2015. THORN was created as a single edition chapbook in winter 2016 during Jeanne Randolph's workshop "Recycling Psychoanalysis: Images, Narratives, Pre-Owned Ideas" at The Centre for Creative Writing and Oral Culture, University of Manitoba. "Hedge" is a response to Sandra Ridley's "Near, March River." GRIEF SILHOUETTES was composed Christmas 2014 for friends and family in three editions of 10. COMMA is a silent collaboration with my brother's handwritten field guide of prairie grasses, composed while he was in SICU and recovery at Winnipeg's Health Sciences Centre, October 2010 – January 2012.

.

"*Fragments are the husk of a secret.*" Mary Ruefle, "On Secrets: eight beginnings, two ends." *Madness, Rack, and Honey: Collected Lectures.* Wave Books: Seattle, 2012.

"*I sit quietly at my desk ... scraps of sounds work into something,*" Susan Howe, "in (some of) her own (fragmented) words," fragmented and collated by Udo Kasemets in *The Liberties* reading pamphlet, Ryerson University: Toronto, 2007.

"*And (I) remembered in amazement that I could swallow, and I did,*" Mary Ruefle, "Monument," *The Most of It,* Wave Books: 2008.

All images, fragments, handwriting, ephemera and collage were selected, reproduced, altered and arranged from the following sources:

BALD-FACED HORNET NEST. Parker Wetlands, Winnipeg, MB, collected September 2013.

BOTTLE GENTIAN (*Gentianaceaea*). Parker Wetlands, Winnipeg, MB, collected September 2013.

Buchner, Leonard J. *Children's Guide to Knowledge*. Home Library Press: USA, 1965.

EAGLE 'CHEMI-SEALED' TURQUOISE WRITING PENCIL BOX, family archives, (Toronto: 1936).

Everett, Thomas H. *The Reader's Digest Complete Book of the Garden*. Reader's Digest: Montreal, 1966.

Garden Hints for Amateurs (pamphlet). The William Rennie Company, Ltd: Toronto, 1923.

HAREBELL *(Campanula rotundifolia)*. Seed collected from my prairie garden, fall 2014.

Johnston, T. B. and Whillis, J. eds., *Gray's Anatomy, 31st Edition*, Longman's Green: London, 1954.

LINECO SELF-ADHESIVE HINGING TISSUE BOX. Holyoke, USA, 2014.

"LONG LIVE THE WILDCARDS, MISFITS & DABBLERS," a painting spotted from Burnside Bridge, eastview. Portland, Oregon: 2016.

Macnamara, Peggy, *Architecture by Birds and Insects*. The University of Chicago Press: Chicago, 2008.

Meine, Franklin J. *Library of Universal Knowledge: The Practical Self-Educator*. Book Production Industries: Chicago, 1953.

MILKWEED (*Asclepias*). Seed collected from my prairie garden, fall 2014.

Peterson, Roger Tory. "Habitats (Where to Look for Birds)," "Silhouettes of Common Birds" from a half-copy, pages 94–166, of *How to Know the Birds*. Houghton Mifflin Co.: Boston, 1949.

PINK MASKING TAPE. Cantech Ltd.: Montreal, 2015.

SCRIBBLER, LE VOYAGEUR EXERCISE BOOK, family archives, 2014.

Simon, Hilda. *The Splendor of Iridescence: Structural Colors in the Animal World.* Dodd, Mead & Company: New York, 1971.

SHEER BLUE FLOWER CURTAIN, south-facing study window, Winnipeg, MB.

Still, Kevin. My brother's handwritten notebook of prairie grasses and flowers, 2010.

Zim, Herbert S./Martin, Alexander C. *Flowers.* Golden Press: New York, 1956.

—. *Birds: A Guide to the Most Familiar North American Birds.* Golden Press: New York, 1956.

—. *Insects: A Guide to Familiar American Insects.* Golden Press: New York, 1956.

—. *Moths and Butterflies.* Golden Press: New York, 1956.

PAPERY ACTS – WORKS CITED:

Atwood, Margaret. "The Difference Between Prose and Poetry." *CBC digital archives*, radio interview: September 18, 1968.

Bacharach, Naftali. "A Poem for the Sefirot as a Wheel of Light," *Poems for the Millennium, Vol. 1*, University of California: Berkeley, 1995.

Bachelard, Gaston. *On Poetic Imagination & Reverie.* Spring Publications: Connecticut, 1998.

—. *The Poetics of Space.* Beacon Press: Boston, 1994.

—. *The Right to Dream.* The Dallas Institute Publications: Dallas, 1971.

Bervin, Jen. Jenbervin.com/projects/the-dickinson-composites-series

—. *The Desert.* Granary Books: New York, 2008.

Borson, Roo. *Personal History.* Pedlar Press: Toronto, 2008.

Brand, Dionne. "Statement," *The New Long Poem Anthology, 2nd edition*, Sharon Thesen, ed. Talonbooks: Vancouver, 2001.

Deletang-Tardif, Yanette. "The Alchemy of Imagination". *On Poetic Imagination & Reverie* by Gaston Bachelard. Spring Publications: Connecticut, 1998.

Geddes, Gary. "Gwendolyn MacEwen," *15 Canadian Poets × 3.* Oxford University Press: Ontario, 2001.

Goldstein, Mark. *Form of Forms.* BookThug: Toronto, 2012.

Hall, Phil. *Notes from Gethsemani.* Nomados: Vancouver, 2014.

Hejinian, Lyn. "The Rejection of Closure (1985)." The Poetry Foundation, Essays on Poetic Theory: www.poetryfoundation.org.

Howe, Susan. *My Emily Dickinson.* New Directions: New York, 2007.

Lee, Dennis. "Body Music: Notes on Rhythm in Poetry," *Thinking and Singing,* Cormorant Books: Toronto, 2002.

Lilburn, Tim. "Going Home." *Thinking and Singing,* Cormorant Books: Toronto, 2002.

McKay, Don. "Long Sault." *The Long Poem Anthology,* Michael Ondaatje ed. The Coach House Press: Toronto, 1979.

Page, P. K. *The Glass Air, Selected Poems.* Oxford University Press: Toronto, 1985.

Rilke, Ranier Maria. *Letters to a Young Poet,* trans by K. W. Maurer. Winnipeg Printing & Eng. Co. Ltd: St. James, 1958.

Ruefle, Mary. *A Little White Shadow.* Wave Books: Seattle, 2006.

—. "On Erasure." *Quarter After Eight,* vol. 16. Ohio University Press: Ohio.

Scholl, Betsy. "The Dark Speech of Silence Labouring: Osip Mandelstam's Poems and Translations. *Numéro Cinq,* vol. iv, No. 5, May 2013.

Solnit, Rebecca. *The Lannan Podcasts: Trevor Paglan with Rebecca Solnit, Interview at Lensic Theatre*: Santa Fe, March 19, 2014.

Szumigalski, Anne. *The Word, The Voice, The Text.* Fifth House: Saskatoon, 1990.

Tillman, Lynne. Bookworm Interview: *What Would Lynne Tillman Do?* KCRW: California, July 31, 2014.

Vanasco, Jeannie. "Absent Things as If They Are Present." *The Believer,* McSweeney's: San Francisco, January 2012.

Werner, Marta / Bervin, Jen. *Emily Dickinson The Gorgeous Nothings.* Christine Burgin / New Directions: 2013.

Wiman, Christian. *Stolen Air: Selected Poems of Osip Mandelstam.* ecco: New York, 2012.

Wright, C. D. *The Poet, the Lion, Talking Pictures, El Farolito, a Wedding in St. Roch, the Big Box Store, the Warp in the Mirror, Spring, Midnights, Fire & All.* Copper Canyon Press: Washington, 2016.

ACKNOWLEDGEMENTS

An excerpt of "Papery Acts" appeared in *cv2*. "Rush-Wick," "Vernix Caseosae," "Derma Dream" and selections from "Swarm" and "Comma" appeared in *Grain*. An earlier version of "Scroll" appeared under the title "Mourning Cloak" in *Vallum*. "Spiny Oakworm" won the 2013 *Prairie Fire*/Banff Centre Bliss Carman Poetry Award. *BafterC* published an earlier excerpt from "Comma" titled "-let". Thank you to the editors.

"Scroll" was suspended in full length at Crescent Fort Rouge United Church in March 2015 for the Arts for Transformation Festival.

Thank you Manitoba Arts Council Deep Bay Artist's Retreat for cocooning time in 2012 and 2013 and the Winnipeg Arts Council for financial support.

Thank you BookThug – Jay, Hazel, Ruth – for making space for "the frail and vulnerable, rare and obscure, impractical, local and small."

Tremendous thanks to Phil Hall and Mark Goldstein for raising the net, catching the *m*, and holding, so carefully, the impossible flutter.

Comma – my long pause – could not have been formed without the steady hold of Darren, Abby, and Ben; Mom, Dad, and Kev.

Dear friends, translators of silence – *long live the wildcards, misfits & dabblers* – this is for you.

A NOTE ON THE TYPE

Typeset in Adobe Minion Pro. Minion is an Adobe Originals typeface created by Robert Slimbach. Minion is inspired by classical, old style typefaces of the late Renaissance, a period of elegant, beautiful and highly readable type designs.

COLOPHON

Distributed in Canada by the Literary Press Group: www.lpg.ca
Distributed in the USA by Small Press Distribution: www.spdbooks.org
Shop on-line at www.bookthug.ca

Type+Design: www.beautifuloutlaw.com
Edited for the press by Phil Hall

ABOUT THE AUTHOR

Jennifer Still's first collection, *Saltations*, was nominated for three Saskatchewan Book Awards. Her second collection, *Girlwood*, was a finalist for the 2012 Aqua Books Lansdowne Prize for Poetry and the first-prize winner of the John V. Hicks Manuscript Award. That same year, she was awarded the John Hirsch Award for Most Promising Manitoba Writer, and in 2013, she won the *Prairie Fire* / Banff Centre Bliss Carman Poetry Award. Still has served as faculty for the Banff Centre for the Arts and Creativity Wired Writing Studio and is a poetry editor for *CV2*. She was the 2015 University of Winnipeg Carol Shields Writer-in-Residence and the 2017 Writer / Storyteller-in-Residence at the University of Manitoba's Centre for Creative Writing and Oral Culture. She lives in Winnipeg.